EMMA CHAPLIN

Winning The Fight

Copyright © Emma Chaplin 2022

All rights reserved. No part of this publication may be reproduced, distributed, or transmitted in any form or by any means, including photocopying, recording, or other electronic or mechanical methods, without the prior written permission of the publisher, except in the case of brief quotations embodied in critical reviews and certain other non-commercial uses permitted by copyright law.

Chaplin, Emma
Winning **T**he **F**ight
ISBN 978-1-922803-80-1 (paperback)

Typesetting Adrianna Regular 9/16
Front cover picture by Melissa Alagich,
Melissa Alagich Photography.
Book edited and designed by Green Hill Publishing

Acknowledgement...

THANK YOU TO MY FAMILY and friends for supporting me during this journey and loving me for who I am. Thank you to my beautiful Mum Liliana for never leaving my side. I could never have gotten through it without you by my side. Thank you to my Dad and brother for your loving support.

I would also like to thank the Serbian community for organising a fundraiser for my family and I in the middle of this difficult journey. A heartfelt thank you to you all for your incredible generosity.

A special thank you to all the doctors and nurses at the Women's and Children's Hospital, Michael Rice (Oncology) Centre and a heartfelt thank you to Neurosurgeon Cindy Molloy and her team for saving my life with your blessed hands. To my Oncologist Ram Suppiah and Martin Borg (Radiation Oncologist), thank you for your knowledge in life saving treatment.

God bless to those who we have lost, survived and who are about to start their journey with cancer.

Let's kick cancer's butt once and for all!!

TABLE OF CONTENTS

CHAPTER 1

In the beginning...

1

CHAPTER 2

Waiting game

19

CHAPTER 3

Round one begins

27

CHAPTER 4

Tough times ahead

37

CHAPTER 5

Make-A-Wish

45

CHAPTER 6
First day of school
55

CHAPTER 7
Stepping up (high school)
63

CHAPTER 8
Canteen
71

CHAPTER 9
My dream job
75

CHAPTER 10
A mother's instinct (Mum's story)
79

CHAPTER 11
Winning The Fight
85

In the beginning...

Tuesday 24 April 2007

IT WAS THE 24TH OF April 2007, Anzac Day eve, when not only my life but my whole family's life was turned completely upside down. The news was horrifying. All I can remember is sitting on my dad's lap and bursting into tears. Even though I couldn't quite comprehend what was happening, I knew it wasn't good as Mum, Dad and my older brother were also crying and were distressed. Nothing made sense, not one word that anyone was saying. It was as if time had frozen and you couldn't hear anything, and all you could see were the doctors' mouths moving up and down.

Six weeks earlier...

Before the nightmare that unfolded, my life was normal. I was a bright, bubbly seven-year-old girl, just about to start year 2. I was so excited as I loved school. Not only did I love being with my friends but I really enjoyed school itself and did well at almost all my subjects except for maths, which I always struggled with.

It was almost the start of a new school year and that meant a trip to get new stationery items. Oh, how I loved the smell of fresh stationery! I remember chucking in the trolley things that I probably didn't even need, but I especially couldn't resist the brightly coloured glittery pens. And not to forget the essential book contact designs: I remember finding it hard to choose, but I finally decided on a ruby red glittery one for that year, which gave Dad a fun job of covering my books.

During the school holidays, my brother, (who was nine at the time) and I would stay at our Baba and Deda's (Grandmother and Grandad) or at our Nana's house, as Mum and Dad worked full time. It was always a fun time at my Baba and Deda's as five of our eleven cousins also used to stay there for the same reason. We used to run amok, racing around the house playing chasey and other random games we made up along the way. To keep ourselves entertained, we also watched movies and played PlayStation, which we brought with us.

Lunchtime was always a good time at Baba's as she would make a delicious Serbian dish or order something from the fish shop. I loved those days as they were so much fun.

When staying at Nana's, we used to go bowling or to the swimming centre with her cousin's grandkids, which was always fun and exciting. During the warmer days we would go down to the beach and grab an ice cream: boysenberry was always a winner for me.

It was during this time that my mum joined me up at a tennis club, which I attended on a regular basis. I loved tennis and watched the Australian Open on TV, always pretending to sign my signature on the camera and hoping to be a top player someday. During this time, I was becoming quite good at it, with my serves and strength. My brother would also come along with Mum to watch and collect the balls for the club. At the end of each session, I remember getting some lollies for every so many points you received during training. My brother got some too, for being the ball boy.

To keep active my brother and I also joined a jiu-jitsu class, which we attended weekly and Dad took us there. I enjoyed it but not as much as I enjoyed tennis, although my brother did well and ended up getting a gold medal for the Brazilian pacific tournament, for which we went to Melbourne in 2006.

On Sundays it was our family day out, and we always went out to watch my brother play soccer, no matter if it was rain or shine. I really enjoyed watching him play soccer, and not only for all the hot chocolates I got. I also loved the sunshine and seeing him going out and doing what he loved. I still remember the cheer song they used to sing when they won ZIGGA ZAGGA ZIGGA ZAGGA OI OI OI!

At home we loved playing with our pet dog Rocky. My brother was the one who named him. He was a terrier-shih tzu cross. He was a crazy, fun-loving dog, running around the backyard and barking at the most random things, like the drops of water from the wet clothes on the clothesline and the birds on the tree. He loved jumping on everyone, especially me, and for some reason he would always sniff the back of my head, which I never understood.

Life was great. I was enjoying my outside-school activities, doing well at school, being in the top literacy and reading classes, and loving life as a seven-year-old. I enjoyed spending time with my family and friends, who would often be over at our place as my parents loved to entertain. This ranged from charcoal barbeques to Yiros nights, and watching the footy together. On weekends I loved playing board games with my brother and parents and going on beach drives on hot summer nights were the best. I cherish these memories.

Weeks went on and it was the start of a new school year. It was a very exciting first day as we had a new principal but getting organised into our new classes was always an anxious time as you were hoping to be in the same class as your friends. I was happy and relieved as I was put in the same class as my friends who I have known since kindy.

I was enjoying learning and being in year 2, but it was then the headaches started. I remember getting home from school and Mum asked me why my left eyelid was blue. Dad had a look as well, but all I could say was, "I don't know". It looked as if there was a thick blue varicose vein sitting there on my left eyelid.

Mum took me to the doctors as she was concerned. He asked me, "Have you been hit by a ball?" I knew I haven't been. He sent us home, with no explanation of what it may have been.

A week passed and I remember my tennis coach commenting on how well I was progressing. I was so happy to receive that feedback and Mum was also very proud. After a few days Mum took me back to the doctor as I was having headaches again and she was very concerned, as this was something I had never experienced before, especially with my eye like this, which was worrying in itself. At this stage, the doctor suggested there didn't seem to be anything wrong and sent us home again. This was very frustrating!

It was almost the first week of the term 2 school holidays and I had my 8th birthday coming up in May. I remember telling Mum and Dad that I wanted a *Bratz* theme party with some friends from school, as I loved *Bratz* and everything *Bratz*, from the dolls to the video game.

A couple of days later, I told Mum my head was hurting again as she picked me up from school. She again took me straight to the doctor and demanded to see a specialist. Mum pleaded, "Please send my daughter somewhere to be checked even if it's just for my peace of mind." He finally did.

On the day of my appointment I was thoroughly examined, which involved balancing and eye coordination tests. At the end of the examination, the specialist seemed a bit concerned, and an MRI scan was booked two weeks later for further investigation.

After my appointment Mum bought me the *Pink 'I am not Dead'* CD I had been begging for days before, having heard the songs at my older cousins house.

At this point I was frightened about what was going to happen. As a kid I thought I was going to get stuck in the machine or something, so I was completely scared. Don't get me wrong, I was also scared of what they might find in the scan as well.

Upon getting home from the appointment, not long after Dad got home from work, I remembered telling my parents that I was scared of the scan and started to cry. They reassured me that it would be fine, but I knew they were also scared.

After waiting weeks for the MRI booking, the symptoms started to become worse and I began to lean on people because of my balance, but I didn't think much of it.

Meanwhile life continued and we were invited to my cousin's 21st birthday party on the 28th of April. I was so excited as Mum took me shopping to buy some new clothes and shoes for the night.

When the day came for the MRI scan it was the school holidays and I remember spending the day at my Baba's house with my brother and a couple of my cousins.

Having the privilege of being brought up in a large family has always been special to me, so being able to spend time with five of my eleven cousins was always fun. During the day, I really didn't think about the appointment as I was too busy playing PlayStation and watching movies with my cousins.

It was about 4:00pm when Mum and Dad came to pick us up. Before we left, I had to change as I wasn't allowed to wear any metal clothing or accessories during the

MRI scan. I clearly remember wearing a red top with white polka dots and black leggings. Once I was ready, we waited a while as my booking was at 7:00pm. I was again reassured by Baba and Deda that everything was going to be okay, and my Deda telling me the time he had an MRI scan and how they are just loud and sound like loud jackhammers.

Soon after, we left for the appointment at the Flinders' Medical Centre. I became more nervous and scared on the drive up there. We hadn't had dinner yet as we ate lots at Baba's during the day. Mum and Dad said, "it wouldn't take long and after we will get Hungry Jacks". Hearing that I was happy, felt a bit calmer and couldn't wait to have dinner.

When we were walking through the hospital I became more nervous and scared as the corridors were dark, gloomy and cold which made me more afraid. We weren't waiting long before my name was called for the scan. I was only allowed one adult with me, so Mum came while Dad waited with my brother. I hugged them both before I went in.

When we entered the room, the machine was already loud and making thumping loud noises like a jackhammer. The Radiologist asked if I brought anything to listen to which helped block out the loud noise, and of course I brought my *Pink 'I am Not Dead'* CD.

When the MRI started I was more nervous than ever but I knew Mum was there sitting close by, so I was a bit more relaxed. During the scan, I closed my eyes and tried to think of something else to distract myself from all of this. The noise was continuous and began to sound louder with different sound patterns. The scan went for about 45 minutes, and I thought 'Great, not long now till we get Hungry Jacks!'

After the scan the Radiologist asked us to wait outside for a moment, and we were taken to a waiting room. A few doctors came to talk to us. I remember sitting on Dad's lap and my brother sitting with Mum. What the Doctors were about to announce would haunt us forever: "We are sorry to tell you this, but your daughter has a brain tumour." After those words were said it was like you couldn't hear anything and you could only see the doctor's mouth moving. I could see my family all in distress and in shock. We were crying and holding each other tight.

The doctors left us for a moment, and we all tried to comprehend what was happening. But I was only seven years old, I really didn't understand—all I knew was it was bad!

Not long after I was transferred to the Women's and Children's Hospital for further care. I was taken by ambulance and Mum came with me, while Dad and my brother drove up and met us there.

When travelling in the ambulance I was so upset and distraught as I was shocked and was afraid of what was going to happen next. I clearly remember the paramedic asking me my name and how old I was and if I had ever been in an ambulance before. I said, "I have once at school when a teacher's husband who was a paramedic came to demonstrate."

When we arrived to the hospital I was admitted and was placed in a room in the Emergency Department. I was in observation which included taking my temperature and blood pressure. They had given me something straight away to reduce any swelling on my brain. It took five weeks from the first-time Mum took me to the General Practitioner (GP) to this moment. Many doctors were coming in to see me and speaking to my parents. It was such a horrendous night. After this traumatic night I finally fell asleep at 12am, after looking at the clock in the Emergency room. Even as I am writing this now and thinking back to that night, I can still feel the fear rush through my body.

The next thing I remember was falling asleep and waking up in a ward, where I stayed for four days while waiting for my operation. Surgeons were quick to operate, and a booking was made for the coming Saturday, which was four days away— the 28th of April.

Every day had a routine; in the morning at 7:00am Dad and my brother would come to the Hospital, then Mum would take him to school while Dad stayed with me. During the day it mainly involved various appointments and board games, arts/crafts, and movies to keep me entertained.

The hospital food wasn't that bad as there was a variety of food. But my favourite was the pizza and of course it was probably the best thing on the menu in comparison to the rest of the food choices.

Friday night, the night before the operation, my aunties, uncles, grandparents and a few cousins gathered in the hospital. We had pizza and soft drinks; I was so happy to have them around me before my major surgery. Who knew what was going to happen to me after the operation? If I was going to be able to talk, walk or even play tennis or go to school again. Too many things could happen. As visiting hours ended I said goodbye to my aunts, uncles and cousins.

I remember Baba saying in Serbian, "I love you sweetheart, I won't see you tomorrow morning, and everything will be okay."

I said "Baba! You must come in the morning. My operation is at 9:00am."

Dad and my brother stayed a little longer with Mum and I after everyone else, as we spent a bit more time together.

Then came Saturday, the day of the operation. It was 9:00am and I was slowly waking up. As I woke, I saw the nurses coming in to prepare me to take me to theatre. All I could see was Mum, Dad, my brother, my aunties and uncles and my grandparents there surrounding my bed. I was so happy to see them before going into theatre.

I said my final goodbyes until coming out of ICU. Saying goodbye to my brother and leaving him behind was hard, because he was my older brother, my protector. We did everything together we had so much fun as kids playing together and who knew what would happen after surgery.

I was wheeled in on my bed with my pink teddy bear I had received during the week. I was so scared and held on to Mum and Dad's hand. I was only allowed one parent, so Dad and my brother kissed me before entering the theatre doors. Prior to the operation the doctors told my parents many things could go wrong, and I may be put in an induced coma for days, for the brain to heal. This was very disturbing for them to hear.

When entering theatre, it was a big cold room with many nurses and doctors. I was even more frightened and didn't stop crying. Mum gave me a big kiss and a hug and said that everything is going to be okay, and she will be with me when I wake up. I remember her saying I love you as I fell asleep. My doctor asked Mum to leave the theatre room so she could begin, Mum turned to them all and said, "I trust you with my daughter."

The operation went for four hours, where my surgeon managed to remove the entire tumour which was the size of a golf ball.

Once the operation was finished the doctor rang Mum and said, "I got it all, Emma is fine and is heading to the Intensive Care Unit (ICU)." Mum repeatedly said over and over, "You got it all, you got it all." The relief was overwhelming, Mum started crying and was very emotional. Mum, Dad and my brother started running to see me in ICU and she forgot to tell the rest of the family I was awake.

Mum stopped, turned back with tears and said, "My girl is fine she GOT IT ALL OUT!" Tears were streaming down her face and there was relief in her voice. Mum said to the doctor, "Your hands are a gift from God to be able to remove the tumour."

When I woke up, I was so sore and stiff, wearing a bandage around my head and a drip in my arm as I was given fluids and medicine. All I wanted was my Mum, Dad, and my big brother. When I heard their voices I was so relieved, and my blood pressure instantly went down and was relaxed.

I stayed in ICU, for several days where I was thoroughly looked after. I was asked to move my neck every hour or so after the four hour long operation and not being moved. The pain was excruciating and there are really no words to describe how it felt, except F***CK or that it felt like a stabbing knife.

On the second night, I was only recommended soft foods like jelly and custard as they had taken the tube out my throat several hours ago. As I had pizza the night before my surgery I was still triggered by the smell and the taste. I demanded it for dinner. The nurse said that I couldn't, but I still got my way a few days later.

After the four days in ICU, I was transferred to a ward where I stayed for two weeks to be monitored and was given pain killers if needed. I was attending physio, Speech therapy and Occupational therapy to regain my strength after the major surgery.

During this time there was a very special day I didn't want to miss out on. My Mum comes from a Serbian cultural background and on the 6th of May it is my Baba and Deda's Saint Day (Saint George).

Saint George is our family's patron saint. This day is also known as Đurđevdan. It's a feast of celebration to pay tribute to Saint George, who we believe is the saint that looks after our family. It is celebrated by our whole family and our closest friends are also invited to celebrate with us. Aside from Christmas and Easter, this is the most religious day for our family. On this day, Baba prepares a huge family feast for us all by making chicken soup, traditional Sarma (cabbage rolls) pork, salads and amazing cakes. Our priest would come to bless the family also.

As I was in hospital during this time, Mum asked my neurosurgeon if I was well enough to go for dinner. She thought about it and said yes as she thought it would be wonderful to celebrate such a beautiful day with my family. She allowed me to go for a couple of hours until 9:00pm.

When I entered Baba's house with Mum and Dad, the look on my Baba's face was priceless and she had tears in her eyes when she saw me. I was happy to get out of the hospital; to be in a different environment. I loved seeing all my family together again and had missed this so much. A couple hours after arriving and having dinner I had a headache and was so tired. I could no longer cope with the loud noise, as my head and ears were sensitive, so I returned to the hospital.

When we got to the hospital Mum, Dad and I had to wait in the foyer until a nurse came to collect me. Dad kissed me goodbye and went back to my Baba's to be with my brother, while Mum and I stayed at the hospital. I was so grateful for Mum never leaving me alone at night. I knew it was hard for my older brother also, Mum made sure every morning someone was with me, so she went home to prepare my brother for school and dropped him off. This went on for a long time. We were lucky to have so much support. Baba and Deda came early in the morning to our house when Dad went to work. Mum would leave the hospital when nana arrived and would take him to school. My Tekta (Mum's sister) was amazing also, attending appointments and taking care of me. She was Mum's rock!!

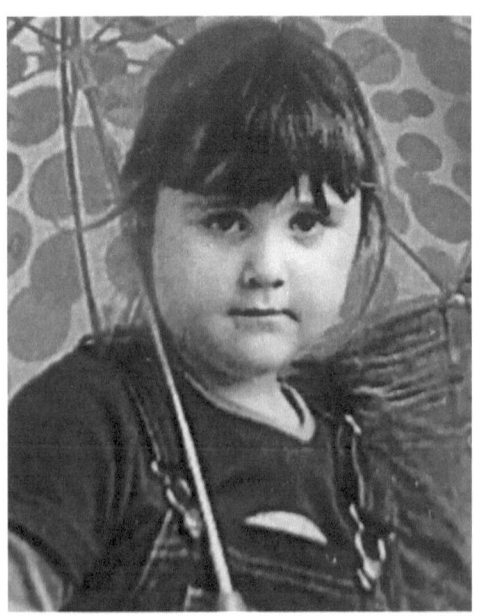

Waiting game

I STILL DIDN'T HAVE A full understanding of what was going to happen, but I just went with what the doctors said and what Mum and Dad told me.

A couple days after returning to the ward I was able wash my hair, which was sticky and rough due to the blood and not brushing it during the period of the operation and time spent in ICU. It was also a coincidence as the nurse who took care of me in ICU in the past four days, returned to the ward after so many years and I was one of her patients, which was a blessing in disguise.

I remember that Mum was a bit hesitant to wash my hair as she was worried she may hurt my head as my scar was 10cm long with too many stiches to count at the back of my head. My neck was also still stiff and sore. I remember the nurse was so gentle; the nice warm water on my hair and the shampoo felt so nice and smelt lovely after such a traumatic couple of days.

The next day Dad and my brother came to spend the whole day at the hospital. Mum and my brother went to the shops (Mum wanted to spend some time with him) while Dad stayed with me and we watched a movie. When they came back, they brought me two *Bratz* dolls which was my favourite and my brother got some wrestling figurines. We spent many hours as a family in the hospital, supporting each other. I had so many visits in hospital from my family and friends. It was lovely to see everyone again, as the fear of the operation was very overwhelming.

My brother went back to school the week after. Dad would come to the hospital in the morning as he took some time off and Mum would take him to school and go home to get what she needed. At the back of my mind, I thought how hard it would have been for him to go back to school after this traumatic couple of weeks.

Instead of me attending school with my brother, I attended Speech therapy as all my left side was affected due to the location and pressure of the tumour. The removal caused damage to my seventh cranial nerve, which left my eye droopy and my smile uneven as my nerves were damaged. I was so upset and cried that I couldn't be with my brother and friends—I was in hospital with no escape. THIS MADE ME SO ANGRY AND SAD.

I was given physiotherapy to get me up walking to see if the operation affected any mobility, but fortunately it didn't at this stage. I also received Occupational therapy to improve strength in my hands. This was done by completing some fun activities such as crafts like using scissors etc.

Then came the day of the Oncology appointment to hear the results of the biopsy. I remember walking into the clinic with Mum and Dad, being so drained and tired and thinking that I hope I didn't have to visit this place again as seeing so many unwell kids while sitting in the waiting room made me sad.

My name was called, and these were the very few last seconds that would change our lives again. We were all anxious and fearful of what we were about to be told by the Oncologist, then he gave us the unthinkable, heart-wrenching news. He announced with sadness that the tumour was an aggressive form of brain cancer called Medulloblastoma, which is located on the cerebellum on the lower part of the brain and can affect balance and coordination. At the time, it was mostly common in children under the age of eight.

We all just froze for a moment until we could comprehend the news. We all broke down and he gave us a bit of time together before explaining my treatment plan.

In the following days my parents had many meetings with the Oncology team, although I didn't hear any of this as I was waiting in the waiting room. I remember being so exhausted and leaning on the couch in the waiting room.

It took me some time to comprehended this...

WTF I HAD CANCER!

The days continued as normal, with general observations and therapy. I remember the physiotherapist using an electric shock-thing to restart the nerves on my face. At the time, I just went with it but now that I think about it WTF was she thinking, my nerves are damaged and how would that fix it? Although I was given Occupational therapy to regain strength in my hands, I found it fun and enjoyed it as I loved cooking and arts and crafts. It reminded me a bit of being at school.

During my hospital stay several family and friends came to see me including my grandparents, uncles and aunties and of course my cousins. My Tekta (aunty) was always by my Mum's side, she was an amazing strength for her. She helped Mum tell the family about the horrible news that night as Mum just couldn't say the words as she was so distraught and in shock. My aunty said she was devasted when mum rang her, and she found inner strength to call the family on Mums' behalf. It would have been the most heartbreaking and difficult phone call. I don't think Mum can find the words to explain how thankful she was that night.

The next day when the doctors did their rounds my neurosurgeon assessed my walking, made some observations and asked how I was feeling. I felt good and was looking forward to Occupational therapy that afternoon as we were going to make cupcakes. After three weeks in hospital my surgeon said I could finally go home. I was so excited for my 8th birthday on the Saturday. YAY! I was finally going to be home. I kind of think looking back Mum may have mentioned to her my birthday was coming and it would be awesome for me to be home.

I was told to go home and recover from surgery for six weeks, as I knew the fight of my life was about begin...

Dad and my brother came to pick us up from the Hospital, I remember inhaling the fresh air as I exited the hospital and how free I felt. When we arrived home Baba and Deda were there. Baba had the house spotless, and my room cleaned, filled with all the gifts I received over the last couple of weeks. The house smelt like home; I loved the smell walking through the house. It was way better than the plain hospital smell I had smelt over the weeks. I couldn't wait to go outside to see my dog Rocky. When I went outside, he jumped all over me and he didn't stop wagging his tail (interestingly, he no longer sniffed the back of my head). I was so happy to be home.

The following Saturday I had my birthday party at home with some friends from school (I was so blessed that they still accepted me for who I was), and a few cousins and aunties. It was set out with a *Bratz* themed cake and balloons, I had a great day playing pass-the-parcel, musical chairs and pin the tail on the donkey. Oh, how I miss childhood sometimes!

For the next six weeks I had lots of rest and visitors popping in, and went for many walks to get fresh air and help with my mobility. I remember Mum taking my brother to school every morning while Dad stayed home with me. Every morning Dad would make me a yummy breakfast and warm hot chocolate, while I would watch my favourite TV shows, such as *Bratz* and whatever cartoons were on.

Round one begins

SIX WEEKS WENT BY IN a flash, and it was now time to start Radiotherapy, which I had every day for six weeks except weekends, with a dose of Chemotherapy, Vincristine every Friday which went for 15 minutes.

During this time, we met with my radiation oncologist and the team, I was frightened because I never thought I would end up here (well I guess no one would ever think they would). The waiting room was cramped with elderly people and I remember there was a bowl of mentos on the coffee table. Ahh if only it was the fruit one as I am not a fan of mint.

Where I received my radiotherapy I was one of many young children attending an adult treatment clinic. The nurses took really good care of me and were so cool and friendly, they even designed a waiting room just for kids and asked for my help to create it. While Mum and Dad were talking to the doctor regarding my treatment plan, the nurse asked me for suggestions. I wasn't quite sure as I was too focused on what was about to happen next, and I wasn't in the mind set at the time. I just said maybe colourful walls and colouring books. I remember her asking,

"What about a wall with a twister mat?" Now I think that is a bit out there, but she did a good job trying to distract me.

During this time my head was fitted with a mask which was used to line up and trigger the radiotherapy beams in the correct location. I found this so uncomfortable as it pushed against my head and face. During the first dose of radiotherapy treatment I was petrified. Who wouldn't be?! I was left on my own in the room to have the treatment, which went for literally two minutes, but Mum and the nurses could see me through the glass. Of course they couldn't be in the room at the time due to the to the high radiation. When the treatment began, it was a red laser which pointed at my head and spine. This went for two minutes and didn't really bother me as it had no effect or so I thought.

Chemotherapy was to commence on the Friday of that week. I remember visiting the chemotherapy clinic a couple of times. I wasn't sure what to expect as this time we were taken through the clinic, but all I could see was sick children receiving their treatment. I felt very sorry for these kids. Today when I think about it I hadn't really comprehended the reality of having cancer and receiving intense medical treatment. On this day Mum and Dad had a meeting with my Oncologist to discuss further intensive treatment. I waited in the waiting room and remember being really drained from the radiotherapy and nearly falling asleep.

During this time, I also had another operation to insert a port catheter (port) under my skin into the right side of my chest which is normally the size of a 50-cent piece. This was used for inserting a drip for chemotherapy rather than worrying about finding a vein every time which sometimes can be difficult and quite traumatic for young children. Instead they accessed the port that was inserted.

This was my first operation after the removal of the tumour, so I wasn't really scared as I knew what to expect. A booking was made and of course I had to fast. I fasted all day and night which then got postponed for the following morning, so I still wasn't allowed to eat anything. This went on for a total of two days due to emergencies and I was obviously starving. When night time came they said it was postponed for another day. So, Mum said that's enough and got me something to eat, but by that time I had already fallen asleep. Finally, the next day I had the port inserted with no complications. It was very weird though, as you could see the port protrude through my skin.

Every Friday after radiotherapy I had chemo treatment. It was a small fifteen-minute dose, but it was a strong drug. I become very fatigued from radiotherapy and chemo over those six weeks.

For the chemo treatment the nurses accessed the port that was inserted. It was first cleaned with an alcohol swab before inserting the needle and drip. The first time was a bit painful, but I eventually got used to it. The treatment began with a flush through of saline before they started the chemotherapy and then a final flush of fluids. This only took fifteen minutes but was draining and exhausting. It wasn't painful or anything, although the saline fluid was a bit cold.

Radiotherapy continued and towards the end of the six weeks of my radiotherapy I had become exhausted and weak. My throat was all burnt inside due to the high beams, and I remember screaming and yelling at my Mum saying I don't want to go anymore. Today I know how hard it was for her to literally drag me out of bed to finish the radiation. I literally felt like giving up, I didn't want to do this anymore, but somehow, I found the strength to get out of bed to beat this piece of shit called Cancer.

After each radiotherapy treatment I could always smell gas and I remember asking the nurses and Mum, "Can you smell that?" But they couldn't. It must have just been the rays from the beams.

Every Friday when receiving radiotherapy, the nurses made it theme day. Every week would be a dress-up theme, and of course this was to make it fun and to take my mind off things. Some of the theme days I chose was clown day and the colour pink day—even the cool male nurses wore pink.

The day finally came—the last dose of radiotherapy. I was so excited but also so drained and frail. When I entered the room the nurses who cared for me during the six weeks threw me a small celebration with pink balloons and streamers. I started crying, but it was due to several reasons; the excitement and the thoughtfulness of the nurses doing that for me but also because I was in pain. My throat was burnt, behind my ears were burnt as well. I cried with happiness that I was able to finish this difficult and torturous radiotherapy treatment. God bless them for going the extra mile to take my mind off things. I will never forget them.

After the six weeks of radiotherapy I was finished. I was told to have a month off to recover from radiotherapy before starting another round of intense chemotherapy, whilst still having my weekly Friday chemo. The side effects from the radiotherapy were terrible; it burnt my throat, I couldn't talk or eat properly without pain for a while. I had a metallic taste in my mouth for a long time. Even still today when I have my yearly MRI scans you can see the scaring down my back and neck.

Although treatment was over there could be lifelong effects such as ongoing hearing loss, fertility issues and different hair/skin growth. My hair is very thin, and my nails are brittle. I feel robbed as many parts of my body have been affected. Cancer just takes and takes. But on the other hand, I was glad I was able to have the option to receive the treatment and that I had the strength for what was yet to come.

As part of my treatment, my parents were asked if they could give approval for me to follow a clinical trial from America. They asked many questions and wanted to know every detail of what was going into my body.

My chemotherapy treatment schedule consisted of three weeks of chemo then three weeks off for my body to recuperate and my bone marrow to recover, ready for the next round of chemo. This cycle went for 52 weeks. These were very toxic and potent chemotherapy drugs. Unfortunately, from these drugs I experienced side effects which included nausea, loss of appetite, tinnitus (ringing in ears), weight loss and hair loss just to name a few.

I was admitted to hospital for a couple of days after each cycle as it was an overnight treatment and I needed fluids to be flushed through after. Unfortunately, sometimes after treatment I stayed for longer as I needed blood transfusions, platelets and I had high temperatures of 37+. My bloods and platelets at times went to 0 and once I had blood transfusions they perked up again. I totally understand the importance of and why donating blood is vital—it saves lives.

Life continued with chemo treatments, doctor's appointments and blood tests. This all became a routine and part of my young life.

Over time, patches of my hair started to fall off and the decision was made to shave it. I was crying at first, but I knew it had to be done. I was so sad after it was all gone. My Mum's friend (who she has been friends with for over forty years) came over to cut my hair. I could feel my hair slowly coming off and I began crying after seeing myself in the mirror. To see myself without hair was extremely upsetting, as my hair was so long and thick. I looked like a different person and wasn't sure how to react as I was shocked. I would never forget the beautiful words from my brother who was 10 at the time, as he ran past the laundry after playing outside. He stopped, looked at me and said, "You look beautiful, Emma," and then ran off again. It was such a beautiful moment, like a beautiful butterfly hovering over you for those important moments in time that give you a reassurance of hope. I will never forget those words even till this day. I love my big brother.

As days went by more side effects started. I started to lose my appetite which resulted in weight loss and I started to become weak and fragile. My lowest weight was a very thin 25kgs which was very concerning for a child of my age and height.

I started to become weak, not only in my immune system but I struggled to pick up a glass of water and it was noticeable that my handwriting wasn't the neat and tidy print as it was a month ago. To help regain my strength I received some occupational therapy at home, during my sessions we played games like 'tumbling towers'. Pulling the blocks out carefully was difficult as I also had to improve my coordination skills. Eventually after a lot of practice in my daily routine I was eventually able to pick up and pour a glass of water for myself. I am sure a lot of people would think that doesn't sound like much of an accomplishment, but for me it was much more than that as I had just regained some self-independence.

A lot of these sides effects and regaining strength has also taught me not to take the little things for granted and that just because you might think you are struggling remember, someone else out there wishes they had the ability to do what you can do.

Tough times ahead

IT WAS A USUAL WEEKLY check-up at the hospital with my oncologist. I remember walking down the hospital corridors with Mum and Nana, and then suddenly I just fell to the floor!

My Mum was as shocked as I was and said, "What, did you trip over?"

I replied with, "I'm not sure. What did I trip over, as I didn't notice anything on the floor?"

As we explained what just happened to the oncologist he had an immediate, heartbreaking answer. We all knew that this could be one of the side effects but rarely suspected that it would happen to me. A side effect from the Vincristine is difficulty walking and weakness in the legs.

As weeks and months passed, I started to become much weaker and my walking started to degrade. I had severe foot drop and I had to be carried everywhere I went or be pushed in a wheelchair.

The weekends were my escape from the daily hospital routine and my chemo treatment. On Saturdays my cousins would come over which I loved as this kept me company. We would either watch movies, play *Bratz*, bake cupcakes or do something fun. This was also a major part of my therapy and recovery.

On Sunday we would go watch my brother play soccer; I loved being in the sun rather stuck inside the house or the hospital. I would always cheer him on; he was a very good soccer player and would score almost every game. Being able to watch his games made me happy as it reminded me of the good old days before I got sick. Especially those soccer games in the cold, wet and rainy weather with a hot chocolate in hand. Although I had to be careful not to catch a cold. When I was too weak to go outside I still would always watch by sitting in the car and beeping the horn when his team scored.

During this time, we met two beautiful, special families. Their daughters were going through cancer treatment at the same time, even though it was the most terrible time of our lives, we were truly blessed that our families crossed paths. As fate was to have it one of the families' sons just started playing soccer in my brother's team. The girls and our mums all became extremely close. The six of us girls were very close, I don't think Mum and I could have gone through this dark time in our lives without their support and understanding.

After going through something like this you have an intense fear going through cancer treatment alone and having someone with us through these times and helping each other understand blood counts, treatments etc was so important. I will be forever grateful to have met two amazing families, the three of us girls were cheeky in the hospital—we developed a bit of reputation there.

We played a few tricks on the doctors to keep them on their toes. I put red lipstick on my lips as I tried to trick the doctor that my blood count was normal and I didn't need a blood transfusion. It was fun but didn't fool them.

Our hearts were broken when our dear beautiful friend Lucy passed away 10/06/2020. Forever in our hearts never forgotten. Our bond is internal, RIP my friend until we meet again xox.

When I didn't have any physiotherapy, chemo treatment or doctors' appointments (which was rare) Mum tried to keep me as occupied as possible by taking me on drives to the beach, Maccas and Hungry Jacks runs (to help me to gain weight), playing board games and playing PlayStation together. I know she let me win most of the times, but she didn't have to as I would win either way. Mum is good at many things but playing video games was not one of them.

We would also go shopping. I hated the stares from people, some would look at me and give me a smile others would just stare for ages. Sometimes I would say to take a picture as it would last longer. Mum would always say they were looking at how beautiful I was.

I also loved *Mr. Bean* as much as I loved *Bratz* and listening to *Pink*. These were the main things that kept me occupied most of the time and was also a huge part of my therapy.

I had many falls when I tried to walk again from the side effects from the Vincristine. I received rehabilitation to help regain my ability. The physiotherapist would come to our house for my sessions. I started off with simple exercises like sitting up and practicing standing up with the support of the physiotherapist and Mum. I remember getting up and being so weak my legs felt wobbly like jelly. I will be forever grateful for all the occupational and physio therapists who helped me get back on my feet.

I also did many leg strengthening exercises to help me stand up and attended hydrotherapy sessions which also helped me get a lot stronger. It took hard work, resilience and determination to get through these sessions and to regain the strength in my legs. My sessions continued with various strengthening exercises, which increased my walking mobility.

I was recovering incredibly well with my walking and gaining weight, I was now able to pick up a glass of water and was able to hold a pencil in my hand. Although there were days when chemo got the best of me, emotionally and physically and where I had to spend multiple hours in hospital to receive blood transfusions after chemo treatment. I had many emotional days; I would cry and reflect on what I had just been through and how I needed to learn to walk again. LIFE WAS SO UNFAIR.

I was exhausted, I just wanted all this treatment to end, I wish I could turn back time, to when I was a normal kid playing and running around. I was so angry and upset.

My beautiful Tekta would also come to most chemo sessions, and she would be Mums' seconds set of ears when the doctors had things to discuss, as Dad had to return to work to support us. I don't think my Mum could have gone through this all without her sister being by her side.

Most times after receiving my chemo dosage my blood counts instantly dropped to 0. As it was a long day of waiting with a lack of blood supply, I had to wait an extra four hours for a bag of blood to arrive to receive a blood transfusion. Lucky I had my cousin with me that day otherwise what else would I do without her to keep me company.

So finally, after the long and gruelling hours of waiting, the blood arrived. I felt a sense of relief and that I would be able to go home shortly. On this day there was a student nurse in the clinic. As I was being hooked up and they prepared the bag, suddenly there was a 'SPLAT!" The nurse split the bag as she put it through the wrong hook. The bag split and the blood went all over my cousin and a bit on me.

We were covered in blood, well B-positive blood to be exact. Could I be exaggerating? The blood was mostly on my cousin and I felt so sorry for her. The student nurse was mortified, but what could we do? We just wanted to get home. So, after waiting another couple of hours for a bag of blood to arrive it was now close to 5:30pm. I finally received the transfusion and my lips and face instantly changed from pale white to bright pink.

We had many visitors during my treatment which I loved: my family, aunties and uncles, my cousins and my school friends. It really helped me get through them visiting. It made life feel like normal. My Mum made sure no one had colds, visitors had to sanitise their hands and there was no kissing me as my blood counts were so dangerously low. My dear uncle Dragan would come and always bring me chicken chips and a bottle of coke. We enjoyed sharing it together.

Always loved, never forgotten, RIP Uncle Dragan 12/03/2017.

After all the perseverance, struggle, pain, awful medicine and treatment sessions we could finally start seeing the light at the end of the tunnel and were almost at the end of my protocol.

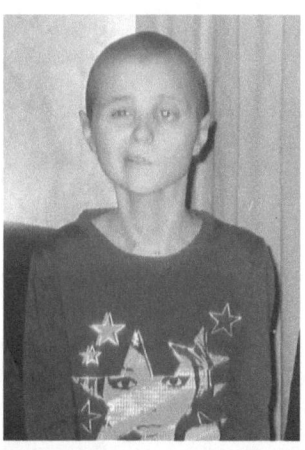

Make-A-Wish

IT FINALLY CAME TIME—THE END of my chemo treatment after 48 weeks. I remember the doctor ringing Mum and saying they would need to end my chemo one month early as my bone marrow could no longer recover. My Mum was reassured I had enough treatment, and they were stopping it. She started crying with happiness; it took her a few minutes to tell me "NO MORE CHEMO!" Once she did I couldn't stop crying either. I was so happy, I could have jumped with excitement. The only thing I had to do was still go every three months for an MRI scan and get my bloods checked, although that was nothing compared to what I just went through. This regularly occurred from every three months then every 6 months and now yearly.

My parents always promised me an end of chemo party and did we party. We celebrated my 12th birthday in style. We invited all the family, my school friends, school teachers, my parents' friends and all our beautiful families from hospital. We had about 120 people, What a moment; all the guests formed a massive circle in the hall, I walked in with the lights flashing and the music was so loud. I walked into the song from *Pink's 'Get The Party Started'*.

OMG, I LOVED IT. I was only using a stick rather than arm crutches. From a wheelchair to this, what a moment in my life. I was so proud of me and all that I had been through. I walked into my own party!

Then it was that part of my journey to make a wish from the *Make-A-Wish Foundation*. A wish is granted to children going through cancer to do or go anywhere they wish. This could be a holiday, to meet a celebrity guest, anything that was wished for.

There were so many things I wanted to do, I was even a bit cheeky to ask for another wish (lol who wouldn't!). Like that was going to happen, only in a child's mind. But the one thing I really wanted to do was go to England to meet *Mr. Bean*. I don't know what it was, after watching multiple hours of *Mr. Bean* I was just obsessed with England, the landmarks, and the British accents. But unfortunately, my wish couldn't be granted as I was too young to travel overseas under their policy.

My next wish was to go to Queensland to go to all the theme parks, *Dream World*, *Movie World*, *Sea World* and *Wet'n'Wild*. I thought this would be amazing as I had never been there before but also to spend time as a family. We had kind of missed this a lot during my cancer journey and I really did miss doing things together as a family.

My wish was granted, we were off to Queensland for a week.

As part of the *Make-A-Wish*, I was in a segment on *Channel 10's Before the Game*. This was a complete surprise and I had no idea. Mum and Dad said to my brother and I that we were going out for lunch, and we just had to wait for a staff member from the *Make-A-Wish* team before we could go. My brother and I were like "okay,"' but we were waiting impatiently. Then the doorbell rang. Mum said we better open the door together so Dad, Mum, my brother and I opened the door. Little did I know it was Fitzy and the Channel 10 camera crew. OMG, my face was filled with such excitement. I turned around to look at Mum and she had tears of excitement in her eyes then I started crying. I was full of happiness and excitement.

Fitzy arrived at our house with a limo where we went to an Italian restaurant in Glenelg and had a pizza cook off and we had dinner. Out of the blue there was Andrew McLeod who brought out our pizzas. They debated who was the best. "Of course, mine was the best, come on Fitzy!" said Andrew.

With winning the challenge, we were off to the Gold Coast and all four theme parks. I loved filming that and meeting them both. It was a memory I would never forget.

It was an anxious and exciting wait leading up to the day of our flight. I had never been on a plane before, nor visited the theme parks. But there was one thing that was holding me back from having the best time possible, and that was the removal of my port.

Finally, the port was out of me. After 48 weeks of treatment, no more FUCKING CHEMO! Last Chemo 8/08/2008. It was not until a few months after I finished chemo when I started to make some huge progress with my recovery.

I was able to walk with the support of a walking frame. My first steps were slow and steady. I felt nervous and was not sure what to do or expect. I was only able to walk from the lounge room to the kitchen, which was not that far but already a huge milestone. The feeling was incredible, and I started to feel a sense of freedom and independence, but I was not finished yet. I was just getting started.

I clearly remember the excitement of helping Mum pack. The night before any of us could hardly sleep from the excitement that was about to come our way. Then the day finally arrived.

Our flight from Adelaide to Queensland was an early one, I remember it was still pitch-black outside when we were travelling to the airport. We caught a maxi cab to the airport and the feeling of excitement was unexplainable.

At this time, I was able to walk short distances with the aid of elbow crutches, however, I still required the assistance of a wheelchair for long distances.

When we landed, *Make-A-Wish* organised with the captain for my brother and I to join him in the cockpit. OMG, what a thrill it was sitting in the Captain's Chair. What a buzz, you couldn't take the smile off my brother's face. We then headed off to *The Mantra* at Broad Beach.

After a good night's sleep it was the official full day of my *Make-A-Wish*. I remember waking up feeling so excited and raring to go. Once we were all ready, we went down for breakfast.

The restaurant choices in the strip of Surfers Paradise were endless, however we chose to have breakfast at the Coffee Club. We ended up going there every morning because I loved it so much. We were handed the menu and OMG, the choices were endless: pancakes, French toast, bacon and eggs... It took me ages to decide, but I had to hurry up because we had a full day planned. I finally decided on a breakfast omelette and course a hot chocolate.

It was scrumptious and I am sure everyone agreed. After breakfast we were off to *Wet'n'Wild*. Oh, how excited my brother and I were, we always remembered how great our cousins made it sound and the many TV advertisements. It was finally coming real. I remember arriving at the theme park and rolling in on my wheelchair. The line was long, but we didn't need to worry about that with our V.I.P passes as we were allowed to enter without waiting.

It was a dream come true, the park was amazing. We didn't know what to do first as there were so much to choose from. We headed to the wave pool, which was a big pool where waves would come every five minutes. I was a bit weaker on my legs at this stage, so I went in with Mum. When the first wave came I think knocked us over; recalling this has brought back some laughs. The next ride I went on was with my brother and it was a ride which was a big splash bucket, followed by go-karts and some more rides and fun. The day was definitely *WET'n'WILD*!

My Dad was a legend during the trip, as whenever there was a ride that had stairs he would carry me up so I could experience all the rides. There was a big water slide that I really wanted to go on which had at least had 50-plus stairs, but he made sure I went on it and carried me up at least five times.

That night when we got back to the hotel I was so exhausted and went straight to bed after dinner.

The next day we went to *Movie World*, again it felt unreal being there in person after watching it on our screens back at home. We bumped into so many characters, *Batman*, *Tweety Bird*, *Superman* and many more. One of the rides I wanted to go on was the *Superman* ride as it looked like so much fun. As I was weak and very light at the time Mum was a bit reluctant for me to go on there, so Dad and my brother went on there first. Lucky, as when they came off my brother was white as a ghost and they made it clear that I wasn't going on that. That was okay, we continued to explore. We reached a middle western themed area where we had lunch, bought some souvenirs, and found some other rides which were bit safer for me.

When we got back, that night we explored the strip of Surfers Paradise. It was such an awesome balmy night with so many lights, I absolutely loved it. We had a lovely dinner at an Italian restaurant and headed back to the hotel to rest for another fully-packed day.

Dream World was next on the list, and this was probably the one I was looking forward to the most as we got to visit the *Big Brother* house. This was awesome as I loved watching *Big Brother*, especially *Friday Night Live*. Entering the house looked so much smaller than it looked on TV. It was such a fun experience. We explored more of *Dream World* and the rides and what it had to offer.

On the last full day in Queensland *Sea World* was the last to be visited, we explored all the animals and sea creatures, and not to forget the cute dolphins. After that we visited a wax museum, it was cool to find celebrities like Michael Jackson and Elvis Presley.

That night when we got back to the hotel we had to pack as we had an early morning flight the next day.

The flight home felt like a long-time home, but it felt good to be home and was a special week spending time as a family together again. It was lovely to get away from hospital appointments, injections, tests, and blood transfusions. It was nice to have the freedom, if only for a short time. Thank you to the *Make-A-Wish Foundation*.

Although it was a wild week away, it was good to be home and see our dog Rocky, when we got home we found him much fatter than we left him, as we had family coming to check the house while we were away and he must have been over-fed.

When we returned from the holiday, a few months later my beautiful godmother (Kuma) came to see us and mentioned how herself, her parents, our priest and a few others in our Serbian community wanted to hold a fundraiser for my family. A few hundred people attended. I felt touched and overwhelmed that so many people wanted to help me and my family during this challenging time and I thank them dearly. I remember people were bidding for a pavlova, paying something like $60 for it and then gave us the money and pavlova. I was so young and wondered how bizarre, but as I'm older I totally understand why. My family and I were so grateful for the Serbian community for gathering for us and hosting a special night. My Kuma was very supportive of us all during this time, I loved her visits with her family and our Yiros nights. She even tried to convince me to be a Port supporter which is her favourite footy team. I did for a year (not sure what I was thinking at the time). Love you Kuma.

First day of school

DURING MY TREATMENT I DIDN'T attend school for multiple reasons: one being that I was vulnerable to infections, and two after receiving treatment I was too sick to even step foot in school. I was always conscious of the port catheter line incision and if I got hit by a ball or something, I don't think it would be a pretty sight not only for me but whoever hurt me.

I didn't attend school for a good two years while receiving treatment and recovering. But I was blessed that one of my school teachers offered to home school me once a week. She was an English/literacy teacher and she helped me stay in touch with my school work and to never fall behind on work—especially when I returned to school.

I remember the first couple of times it was quite awkward having one of my teachers in my home. But I was also blessed at the same time. I am forever grateful for her, and she is a special part of my family, even today.

I was still completing the same work as my classmates back at school: maths, English and Powerpoint presentations. I also was able to complete the NAPLAN test, obeying the same rules and guidelines as everyone else, which I did well at.

After having a year and half off school, it was finally the day to return. There was no doubt that I was nervous as there were so many things running through my head like: will all my old friends recognise me and treat me the same? What about the new kids, will they say anything?

Although this was on my mind, I knew I still had my good friends by my side. I was told that my teacher at the time spoke with the class about my return and explained to the class that I may look a bit different and that I would be bald like him until my hair grew back.

I started to go back to school for a couple of hours a day to get back into the swing of it. Mum worked in the school canteen during this time in case I needed anything, which I rarely did but it was good to know she was there.

I remember the first day back like it was a new year starting school with brand new stationery and uniform. My teacher organised me to sit next to my best friend for the first couple of weeks back, which I was quite happy about.

Although I was happy to be at school, I still did not really feel the same as I did prior to my diagnosis. I was a changed person. I really enjoyed the first day and was looking forward to the next, although I was a bit worn out.

The next day one of the kids came up to me and asked. "So how did you get cancer?"

I froze and I did not know what to say. I wanted to say: why are you so stupid asking me that. I ignored him and went back to my friends. I guess looking back on that now, kids are simply curious, and it was from a lack of knowledge.

Not long after that awkward conversation, the school got in touch with *Camp Quality* to organise a Primary School Cancer education program. The program features the *Camp Quality* puppets which helps educate schools and their students. It also provides a supportive community for individuals impacted by cancer directly or indirectly, such as siblings or parents.

The *Camp Quality* team came to school to hold the program. It was great as the puppets provided a fun and interactive performance, and explained everything about childhood cancer in a way that young people would understand. They answered any questions that students asked. After the performance I felt a sense of relief as students now had some idea about what I was going through.

School was now slowly getting back to how it used to be, but I knew it would never be 100% the same. I was happy to get back into spelling, writing and art, not to mention being back with my friends.

Oh, how I have missed hanging out during recess and lunch time, although it did make me sad because I couldn't run around like I used to. I couldn't play on the playground, monkey bars or play chasey, especially with my walking crutches.

But one thing is for sure, I was grateful that my friends didn't leave me to be alone during recess or lunch. They always made sure that I was still included in what they were doing. This would be through telling jokes, just generally talking about things. We played games that I could be included in. If one friend wanted to run off onto the swings the other would be with me, they would take turns. They were amazing. This was an important part of my recovery to know I was still included and was part of our friendship group.

Each day I slowly transitioned from part-time school to full time hours. At first, I was really drained, my teachers were helpful and very supportive during this time providing homework if needed and extra support.

Days, weeks, terms, and years continued, and I passed my way through primary school. At the end of each term as a treat, a group of my friends and I would go to the local cafe for hot chips and a milkshake, it was well-earned and we made it a tradition.

Throughout all my years of Primary School I found year 6/7 the most difficult but the most valuable years of all. It was probably the most emotional also, as it was the last two years with my childhood friends knowing that we wouldn't be entering high school together.

Year 6/7 was also a very exciting time as we had a brand-new teacher join our school. I remember the first day entering the classroom and it was so organised, each desk for each student had a set of stationery all the same which included a pen, pencil, highlighter, folder and exercise book for each subject. I was thinking to myself wow, and how organised, and this should be a good year. I was in my glory, but even better I was placed on the same desk as my best friends.

Those two years passed by. I was feeling good, having my regular check-ups and MRI scans, and not having many days off. I was exhausted, I was determined to do the best I could to be ready for high school. Finally, it was graduation and the last time I would be with my awesome friends. All the hard work we all put in to get here was well worth it. To celebrate we went on a dinner cruise down West Lakes and returned to the school gym for our graduation ceremony. I remember the lead-up to the big day, the excitement and what to wear. After school when I went over to my best friends' houses, we would always discuss what dress we were going to wear and how we would have our hair. I had so many ideas but thinking about them now they probably weren't that realistic. I ended up finding a nice blue dress and some cute silver flats.

The night of the graduation was so exciting but also very emotional as it was another milestone I had achieved. We had to do a speech to thank everyone for helping us graduate primary school, I thanked my family, Mum, Dad and my brother for all their love and support. I also thanked my grandparents, teachers and my special school friends who were with me every day. I don't think they actually know how their kindness and acceptance helped me heal emotionally after all the trauma I went through. I will be forever grateful.

The next day was the last day of our primary school lives. After the bell rang my friends and I went to the park to celebrate with about seven of us. That night we FaceTimed each other until early hours of the morning, we couldn't seem to let each other go. We now catch up every now and then. I am so blessed they were part of my life during those difficult years. I will always have a special place in my heart for them.

Stepping up (high school)

SO, IT WAS FINALLY TIME for me to start high school, yep, your little Emma is not so little anymore. I will tell you now that I was a bit scared to start high school as none of my close friends from primary school were going to the same school as me, and as I was entering quite vulnerable, with a walking stick and was quite unique to the other students.

I remember asking my brother if there were any bullies or if kids get royal flushes, and of course as an older brother he would tell some white lies but was obviously joking. I know from a distance my brother would observe to ensure I was settling in and to ensure I was okay.

I remember orientation day was a bit scary and only knowing two classmates from primary school. I remember the school having a sausage sizzle that day for the soon-to-be year 8's. My brother and his mates looked after me that day and made sure I got one. I remember him being sneaky and grabbing one for himself as well.

The whole day was filled with lessons such as woodwork, English, music etc which were more trial classes. I couldn't wait to get home as the day was exhausting.

Throughout my high school years I made new friends and excelled at most of my classes except for the usual maths and science which were the classes I disliked the most. My favourite subjects were child studies, English, sports and science, and food and hospitality. Not just as I was in the same class as my friends but also because these were my strongest subjects and I was most interested in them. Oh and these classes had the best teachers, you can't learn without great mentors, right?

Don't get me wrong, I loved school, learning new skills, socialising with friends, and doing all the fun activities School has to offer like excursions and camps. But there was one event that occurred every year which I felt excluded from, which was of course Sports Day. Now don't get me wrong, my primary school was fantastic trying to get me involved in additional tasks when it came to physical education (PE), but I just wanted to run out there with my mates and didn't just want to sit there watching them from the sidelines. That's the part I missed most of my childhood.

This even occurred in subjects like PE, yeah teachers did their best to involve me by blowing the whistle or keeping score and I take my hat off to them but we all know it's not the same. I tried to avoid any Sports Day events for these types of reasons, although I would still support my team.

Sitting on the sidelines continued for years until I was in year 10. It was now 2015 and I was now eight years into remission. This stage in my life I was going well, and I only needed a simple walking stick for support. It was also the first year I was undertaking PE as a subject. The feeling was amazing, and I felt a sense of freedom again. Learning about fitness, nutrition and teamwork was a highlight for me.

The teacher I had was so inspirational; he had an idea of my history as he had my brother for soccer in previous years. He encouraged me to be involved in everything and anything I was interested in.

So, it came to that time of the year again Sports Day nominations. The Sports Day team that I was part of were also very supportive. They involved me in every way possible, even though I sat back a little bit as I wasn't too sure what to say or do.

Then my teacher came around and said, "So Em, what events will you be participating in this year?"

I wasn't too sure how to respond, was I even capable of participating in an event. I responded with, "Well what events can I participate in."

His response was quite positive, "Anything you like, but I would like to see you to participate in at least one."

So, I discussed with my team captain which events were still vacant. Javelin, shotput, sprint race and various others were available. So, I decided to choose Javelin and to participate in tug of war with my team. I felt a sense of relief and excitement coming up to the Sports Day event.

The day finally arrived; it was a stinking hot summer's day. I woke up so excited and energetic, ready to do this thing. Our School held the sports event at Santos Stadium. I remember arriving with a friend as we had to find our own way to the Stadium. As I got out the car, I took a deep breath and inhaled the fresh air, embracing this amazing opportunity I had worked so hard for.

Before taking our places, we had to check in with our home teachers for our attendance, and then the games began. There were three teams Courage (Red), Resilience (green) and Optimism (yellow). I was so pumped and prepared I even coloured my walking stick in yellow.

The day kicked off with novelty events, although I didn't participate in any of these, I was still in the grandstand cheering on with my team. It wasn't till around 11:00am that it was time for the javelin event.

Then it was my turn, I stood a couple metres away for a short run up, I firmly gripped the Javelin and inhaled the fresh air. Off I went; I threw it as far as I could. I repeated this two more times. Although I didn't come first, this EXHILARATING moment will be with me forever. I felt free out there.

Then it was time for the ultimate tug of war, the whole school gathered to the centre of the stadium. The feeling was electrifying, fun and very loud with everyone cheering on their team. What a thrill......

It was our turn, we had to defeat green to make the finals. Our girls were pumped and ready. I took the lead at the front of the rope followed by the rest of the team, then it was war. I held on to the rope with all my strength and determination. I looked down and noticed that the grass was wet from the water events which I thought was a stupid decision doing water events first. Then I slipped. I was determined not to let go, holding on for dear life. It was like a roller coaster ride, I was thrown around but I didn't care. It was finally over... I was lying on the grass. I felt fantastic. I couldn't stop laughing, we all were laughing that was so much fun... What a win; I was stoked. I wouldn't say I am over competitive, but I do like to win, lol.

We had to win another round to collect all the points. I wasn't ready, I was exhausted and it was so hot but I had to do what I had to.

I went in there and on three, two, one the yelling started to win the full set of points. We all started pulling but I don't know what happened, my whole team fell like a stack of dominoes.

Unfortunately, we didn't collect those final points. That was the final event I participated in that Sports Day. The remainder of the day was spent with friends and cheering on the team.

The day was unforgettable and I loved every moment. I could finally say I participated in a Sports Day event since my diagnosis. One of the biggest goals I had ever wanted to accomplish. The feeling was so surreal, and I had a smile on my face for weeks. I was so proud to be part of a team.

That day gave me so much self-confidence and thank you to one special PE teacher!

After five years of many hours of study, stress and unnecessary break downs it was finally time to graduate. Our graduation ceremony was held in town with at least 200 students and their family and friends. I wasn't expecting to get many certificates that night, except for the general year 12 certificate. I ended up getting quite a few from all my subjects, but what was more exciting was receiving the 'Success through diversity' award, and trust me I was not expecting that. When they announced the category they stated 'With their positive attitude and perseverance this award goes to… Emma Chaplin." I was speechless and my peers all turned and the whole audience clapped. I actually don't think my peers quite understood what I went through to get to that point in my life. This was one of the proudest moments of my life.

It just goes to show you can achieve anything if you put your mind to it. And as Mum always told me, "Never let your limitations define you."

Canteen

OKAY NOW DON'T GET ME wrong, I have a great network of supportive friends who care and have supported me but didn't quite get it because they haven't experienced what I have gone through. That's when I decided to join *Canteen*, an organisation for teenagers and young adults who have been affected directly or indirectly by cancer.

It was suggested by my nurse at the children's hospital at my final oncology appointment in the children's system. "You could meet new people in a similar situation who have shared some of the same experiences," she explained. I gave it a thought and decided why not.

After my appointment I jumped online and started having a look at their website, what *Canteen* was about and the different services they offered. I was quite impressed and thought why not give it a go, so I signed up and sent off an email. A couple days after I received an email response and was asked to come into the office for a meeting where I spoke to a counsellor about my journey. Let me tell you there never is a time where I don't break down sharing my story. I don't know what it is, like obviously it's hard, which also kind of takes me back to some dark days.

So, there I was now a member of *Canteen*. I was looking forward to meeting people who would get it, the feeling of understanding what is like to go through something like cancer.

Not long after I was invited to join the Stronger Me program which focused on wellbeing and healthy life choices, which ran for six weeks. I was so nervous when I first arrived, feeling vulnerable, the sense of the unknown and not knowing anybody was so scary.

When I entered, I was a bit lost as to directions. Kindly a *Canteen* member was outside who greeted and welcomed me. I entered the room and obviously was a bit shy. During the session there were lots of team bonding activities which helped me meet the members and new people. By the end of the session I felt like I knew everyone as they were all so friendly and welcoming.

Over time attending events, I decided to be a member of the Leadership program, which is a small group of members coming up and bringing ideas forward for overnight camps, day events etc for members. My favourite part about this was making new friends and bringing my ideas forward, but also the interstate annual meetings held in Sydney. I remember the first time I went; it was so much fun meeting new people from around the country and New Zealand.

I also remember the first interstate camp I went to in Brisbane in 2019, which was at a retreat two hours from the city. As it was an exciting time for me, it was an emotional time for Mum as this was the first time I was going interstate without her. I remember calling her that night and her asking if I was okay. I wasn't too worried about myself, I wanted to make sure Mum was okay!

Although I am no longer a *Canteen* member, I still have made some great lifelong friends which I continue to see today and regularly stay in touch with. One of them being the beautiful member who helped me at my very first session.

My dream job

AFTER HIGH SCHOOL ALL MY school friends started to drift their own ways, starting Uni, and getting part time jobs. I also wanted to gain some independence and responsibility by getting a part-time job, which was one of my next goals. I started to apply for part-time jobs, one of them being as a 'checkout chick'. As a requirement it asked me to fill out some basic questions as well as asking if I had a disability. Of course I ticked yes and then submitted the form. It also asked for which days I was available; I was on holidays and had nothing to do so I put down that I was flexible. A day later I received a response and was rejected. I continued to apply to the same variety of stores, until one day I decided to put down that I had no disability, to see what would happen. Surprisingly I received an email inviting me to an interview.

On the day of my interview, I presented myself well and was interviewed by two ladies explaining my situation etc and advising that I was flexible. The following day I received another rejection letter and the reason was I didn't suit their time of work hours. I thought 'are you serious, did I not just say I was flexible?!' And how is this not discrimination? Anyway, after explaining this to my Mum, there was no stopping her from making a complaint. She picked up the phone and contacted them explaining the confusion. They suggested we contact a disability group; Mum was still very angry the way they handled this.

From here we set up a meeting with Disability Works Australia. The kind lady on the phone told me not to worry about applying for a checkout role. "What are your long-term future goals?" she asked. I said I would love an administration role. They helped me apply for suitable positions which were at different businesses, one of these were within the Government as an Administration Assistant.

After applying for this, I was invited to an interview. The ladies on the panel were nice and very professional; the building was huge as it had 16 floors. I was able to bring along the person from Disability Works Australia as support, who assisted me in searching for this job. As nervous as I was, I kept my cool and thought I did well. In the interview I spoke of my work experience at an aged care facility in the lifestyle department. I really enjoyed interacting with the residents and listening to their life stories. I also worked in administration during school holidays for work experience. I spoke of my hobbies and of course I proudly showed them my Success through Diversity Award.

Two weeks passed by. I was anxiously awaiting a call and finally the day came. I was offered the ASO1 position as an Administration Assistant. I was so excited and relieved! I was offered a wonderful career opportunity, me the girl who was rejected for the checkout position.

My first day was a couple weeks after. On the 12th of February, 2018, like a new school year. I was excited to wear my first corporate-work clothes for starting my new and first job. I was now a public sector employee. The first day was a bit of a blur, meeting new people, setting up accounts and learning procedures.

The past four years have been wonderful; I have learnt and grown immensely, and I have received so much support from my workplace and colleagues. I completed a certificate III in Business Administration at TAFE, a First Aid certificate and had been provided with many opportunities to excel and grow. I am truly blessed and fortunate for the opportunities. I am currently an Executive Services Officer. I will be forever grateful for all my past and present management and staff that have assisted in my development.

A mother's instinct
(Mum's story)

WHEN THE DOCTOR ANNOUNCED, "YOUR daughter has a brain tumour," it felt like my soul literally left my body. The fear was so fierce, ripping us all into pieces. We were all in shock and emotionally confused, hugging each other, crying and not understanding what we have just been told.

The nurse asked me to fill out some paperwork ready for the ambulance to transfer Emma to the children's hospital. With my eyes filled with tears I completed the form. As I walked back to my family, I knew at that moment our lives would never be the same. Taking Emma back to our general practitioner multiple times before she was diagnosed, it was like something deep inside my gut knew something was not right. I remember one night I was watching her sleep, it was as if an inner voice said to me take her back to the doctor again. I think it was a mother's instinct, that little voice we all have. Please never dismiss it, I certainly am grateful I didn't. Our doctor was a wonderful man, he just never expected a seven-year-old otherwise healthy child could have a brain tumour. No one would have expected that to be the cause. Especially not fifteen years ago as brain tumours in children were not that common.

Everyone says, "You are so strong," as a parent of a child going through cancer. We may appear strong, but we are far from it. We pretend to be strong so our child doesn't see the utmost fear in our eyes, and that at any moment it could be the last moment with your child.

Emma had many months of chemo and radiotherapy, she had endless blood transfusions and many surgeries. Over the years her body has been knocked about at every angle. I prayed every night, that my daughter would get through her treatment without pain.

One night I dreamt of two bearded men in white coming towards Emma and myself as we were walking. I was holding Emma's hand on my right side. They stopped and spoke to me and said, "Don't worry, everything will be fine, she will get better." I turned and replied, "I'm sorry, but I need to hear this from God." They said for me to look to the right, and next to Emma was a beautiful bright light shaped as a dome. At that moment I woke, gasping for air with tears in my eyes. I knew when I woke God was with us. I know many would say it is just a dream but I am holding onto it, as my hope.

Over the past 15 years, Emma has endured 2 facial surgeries to help her fully smile, unfortunately unsuccessfully (caused from the tumour sitting on her facial nerve) each operation lasted 10 hours, and now

15 years after treatment ongoing hearing loss and now wears hearing aids and is checked every 6 months due to Radiotherapy late side effects. A gold weight was inserted in her eye to help her blink. 2 calf muscle operations to stretch her legs to help her walk. Botox inserted in her legs to help release the tightness in her calf muscles, to help improve her walking, which has been a wonderful improvement, especially this past year.

My heart is broken that my beautiful girl has gone through such a traumatic, horrifying experience in her young years.

As a mother of a child who had cancer, yes, I'm angry. My daughter missed out on her childhood years and had to spend many of those years in hospital. I'm angry that my daughter could not run and play like other kids. I'm angry as a young adult she couldn't go dancing freely or enjoy a few drinks without people thinking she was drunk due to her being unbalanced. I'm angry she missed out on a lot of things.

I am angry that cancer has taken so many lives.

We may look strong but believe me our hearts and souls are on fire with pain that no one can see. We are all allowed to be angry, we are allowed to cry.

It is vital that anyone going through cancer have a range of supportive groups of family and friends. It is part of the healing process. It is good to have someone that will just sit and listen to your fears and just let you talk.

I have always taught Emma, "Never let your limitations define you." She has definitely not let that happen. Emma has many achievements, which have all come from determination, diligence and an empowered will to become who she is today.

I feel proud that my beautiful daughter is becoming the woman she was meant to be.

Emma is an old soul; her love and light shows through her beautiful blue eyes and warm angelic voice.

I am so proud to have been chosen as Emma's mother. I would like to express my heartfelt thank you to all who have crossed Emma's path over the past fifteen years. Even to this day, everyone in her life has made an impact on her recovery, healing, and growth.

Love to you all, and God Bless.

Winning The Fight

I HAVE BEEN THROUGH A lot for someone so young. One thing that my Mum would always say to me is, "Never let your limitations define you." I don't, I am me and this is who I am.

Sometimes I think of how far I have come. If I am listening to a mellow song or a song I listened to during those tough times I have vivid flashbacks to those dark days. I sometimes get a little bit emotional and upset as the lyrics in a song resonate with me.

I guess I will always have in the back of my mind, why me? Often, when people say if you had one wish what would it be, most would respond with money or fame. But if I had one wish it would be to get rid of this horrible disease and wish that it never existed. It impacts everyone, not only the individual, but it is also very cruel to watch someone going through a situation like this.

Today after fifteen years in remission since my diagnosis of brain cancer I am viewing my journey and the experiences I faced with the most positive perspective by focusing on what I can change not what I can't. I hope that by sharing my story I give hope to others.

All the challenges I have experienced and all the people I have met through this journey have played a huge role, no matter which chapter they entered my life. The quote: "hard times will always reveal true friends," has been defined throughout the last decade and a half of my life. I am forever grateful to all my beautiful friends that are and have been in my life. Especially my bestie who I met in my teen years. She makes me laugh and loves me for me. Every time we are together, we dance, sing, go for town drives and just let loose. I can be my crazy self.

I remember one time we went to the adult shop as we were curious young adults. As we got in the car to leave the car decided to not start and I had to call RAA. It was so embarrassing to state the location and I tried to sugar-coat it by saying that it was the safest place we could pull into. When the road assistant arrived, the old man was not impressed. This was just one crazy adventure. I am forever grateful for her friendship.

The date of the 24th of April, 2007 (the night before Anzac Day) will always be an important date to not only me but all my family and friends who have supported me through this difficult, emotional, and unknown journey.

Being diagnosed with brain cancer at the young age of seven has been the most daunting time of my life to date. I entered the darkest tunnel, not knowing what to expect, but in the end there has been light. The goals and achievements that I have overcome, from learning to walk, talk and complete daily tasks like holding a glass of water, to smashing all my goals and having my dream job. Every year when this date comes around I reflect on these accomplishments. Of coming out stronger than ever. It has been one of the greatest gifts that I have received. But also thinking of the people involved who have supported me throughout my journey to become the strong individual I am today.

I have met some incredible people along with my family who I love dearly and will cherish for the rest of my life. This journey has made me a stronger person in all aspects, physically and mentally. Never ever give up on your dreams, and it is true when they say, "You don't know how strong you are, until being strong is your only option." At the start of this journey, I wasn't sure of what to expect and I tell you I never expected having 12+ operations, countless blood transfusions, being wheelchair bound. I have gone from having a walking frame, to walking sticks and now I barely have to depend on a walking stick.

Without challenging work, dedication and support from doctors and loved ones, I have no idea where I would be today. One thing I can say is that I am truly blessed to be here and very grateful for those who have been part of my life.

Never underestimate the power of family, love, faith, hope and the strength of your inner soul.

Today, after my journey and all the experiences I have encountered, this has made me have a completely different perspective on life. It is indescribable. I will never be 100% the same I was before I was diagnosed, which I understand and now can accept as the new me; which is sassy, sweet and above all I am beautiful in my unique way.

Like Mum has always said, "Don't let your limitations define you."

God bless to those we have lost and those who are fighting today, amen!

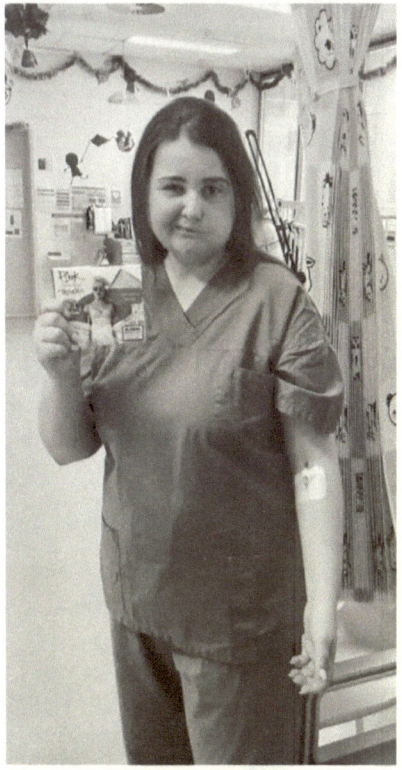

www.ingramcontent.com/pod-product-compliance
Lightning Source LLC
LaVergne TN
LVHW040157080526
838202LV00042B/3207